Come Walk with Me:
Poems reflecting walks around Devon

Annie Jenkin

Dedication:

For my special friends who have provided support, encouragement & inspiration on my walks and poetry journey.

FOREWORD

When Annie Jenkin averred to me her excitement at the prospect of publishing her first collection of poems, *Come Walk with Me: Poems Reflecting Walks Around Devon,* I felt her excitement. In fact, the only person who comes close to that same excitement is the writer of this foreword! For approximately five years, Annie and I have worked closely on many of these poems. She has been a regular contributor to the highly regarded online poetry journal, *Quill and Parchment*. As editor of Q & P, it has been my singular pleasure to observe her maturation as a poet. While I occasionally comment on her work, offering suggestions where I think such are needed, Annie's development is the singular achievement of her own tenacity and commitment to writing excellence.

It has been said that the most important quality of good poets is not skill, *per se*, nor is it a "good ear" for rhyme, as some would have it. These traits and more are easily observable in Annie Jenkin's work. No, the most important trait of good poets is *love*. Annie loves Devon and the sea and Plymouth; she loves the natural world about which she writes with a gifted pen. From "Pleasurable Pastime," "My heart soars / as I taste tangy sea air / blowing towards me." Her love compels her to include many interesting details in her poems, "the busy claws of a badger's raking / out hollows in the night's darkness."

One of the most influential poets of the last century, Wallace Stevens, once wrote, *Poetry is a response to the daily necessity of getting the world right.* As I read the poems in Annie Jenkin's debut collection, I noticed that she is doing more than simply writing poems *about* nature, she is nourishing the human spirit by blending those qualities she finds in the natural world, with the impulse in all of us to get the world right.

Michael Escoubas

Editor, *Quill and Parchment*

Contents

Pleasurable Pastime

When my anchor drifts
aimlessly along,
I slip on my boots
and take a long-awaited walk
tramping through narrow lanes.

Passing bottle-green ivy
and pale shoots of nettle
below budding blackthorn.
Admiring how purple periwinkle
and vivid wild violet colours
clash with golden gorse
telling us spring is finally here!

My heart soars
as I taste tangy sea air
blowing towards me.
It's exhilarating to see
sprawling rocks stitched
to the sea by a stream
of endless white surf,
row upon row trying
to take hold of the shore
fray and slip away.

Beyond the estuary
a sailboat pulls about
watching dolphins play,
fulmars cackling, seagulls

glide, squawking to all.
What a blessing
to live by the sea.

When I walk

I see how a weir can be silenced
by the twists and turns of a river's course
and how this stillness can be broken
by rings of life, as fish pause for breath
or bending reeds reveal
the way a current flows.

I check the ground
to see imprints of a gallop;
the busy claws of a badger's raking
out hollows in night's darkness.
The weariness of tree roots
made shiny by heavy foot-fall
or the oak that cracks and drops
a branch without reason -
except for its aging.

How sunlight shines
through dandelion clocks
as if footlights for butterflies
to flutter, dance or pirouette
then settle for a brief rest.
The iridescent beetle's back
tracking its way through grass
or across a hazardous path,
where a thrush searches
for twigs and wool, and who
might forsake its nest
for a tasty treat instead.

At bright new leaves nudging
prisms of chestnut blossom
or carpets of pink and white
which lift as one in a breeze
to tumble down the field
tickling bluebells as they pass
complementing wild sorrel
or sticking to vivid violets.

When I walk, there is time
time to rest and absorb
my journey's pictures.
Time to pause and wonder
at these precious gifts.

Jenny's Home

Once appearing
on an English farthing,
her singing is famous
from sunrise to sunset
throughout the year.

Wearing a feathered jacket
of reddish brow
with painted cream eyebrows
she might be hidden
amongst the hedgerows,

brambles or ivy,
but also look up
into the fork of a tree
for a domed lodge,
all twigs and moss.

Tiny jenny wren
the cave dweller
who builds a dozen,
choosing only one
to last all summer.

Scouring undergrowth
searching log piles
in crevices and cavities
for insects, beetles
ants, spiders and flies.

Like a small brown ball
flying over the ground,
beating little wings
making a whirring sound,
opens its feathers

in parachute form
gliding gently down,
nestles in its quarters
fluffs up its quilt
and falls fast asleep.

The Himalayan Gift

Tiny green flames flutter
like butterfly wings
to shoo away the gloom
of winter blues,
signalling the arrival
of an ancient Himalia gift,
the cherry blossoms.

This soft, calming white joy
with five little petals
promising renewal
a symbol of love,
greets my spring day.
It gives me time to reflect
to treasure its display.

A flurry of wind frees
and lift petals skyward
like a melee of paper boats
swirling in a snow-globe,
lining my pathway
a living light of hope
that summer swallows
will soon follow.

Springtime in Plymouth

Sun rays glow on plush moss-
this rich blanket grows on a tree stump,
when a squirrel hops on, it's as if
he is regally seated on a throne.

watching a gold crest dither
and flit until spotting a prize.
It lands, hangs upside down
to pluck a tiny caterpillar.

I pause mid-stride, and gaze
at a chestnut brown coat, standing
so still. A young doe with ebony eyes
stares back, suddenly she bolts.

Perhaps, spooked by a blackbird
loudly rustling leaves, flipping
them over, flashing an orange beak
triumphant, he wings away.

My ears are drawn to a noisy crow,
protective of young; he harries and pesters
a buzzard who barely flaps a wing
gliding out of sight over tree tops.

Early bluebells sway in the breeze
their scent draws a brimstone,
bright yellow wings shimmer against
rich new greens adorning a river bank,

where water jumps and gurgles
as if tickled by its pebble bed,
running below a Victorian viaduct
that echoes of a bygone era.

High up on a rocky ledge
peregrines nest in an old quarry,
one sits on the clutch, the other waits
in the sunshine for new life to arrive.

I feel an affinity here...
nature's heart open to all,
this freedom to explore
thrills me to the core.

Sapphire Snow

Dear Robin,
I'm coming down your way today. My curiosity
is peaked as to how you are getting on.
You look terrific in your smart red vest
going from branch to branch of your territory,
and so quick off the mark sending out alerts.
But I worry, in case you have been dismissed
from your post again this year.

Do you get mad at your competition?
Formally dressed in his black suit,
I'm sure his tailor starched his tail. It sweeps
down, sleekly complimentary to his posture,
gliding smoothly over shoulders and head.
Though your cords are very distinctive.
If I might be so bold, it appears to my ears,
he does have a wider range of songs.

The trees dressed in fresh leaves look magnificent,
and begin to spread their canopy,
as if protecting all below,
and what of the bluebells amassing on the slopes?
In the evening, their beautiful scent drifts,
like whispers floating by on the breeze.
The volume of sapphire hue is stunning,
giving the woodland a truly magical feel.
Have you ever heard the bells tinkle
or seen the fairies coming down to choose
their bonnets for the Spring ball?

It is such exciting times now, so many new
things to see and explore.
I'm looking forward to you telling me more.

Sincerely yours.

Devon's Wild Walkway

Bitter biting winds
bluster across the headland
lashing fast the twisted trees,
and tufts of fur and fleece
flutter on thickets of gorse.

As fallen bracken and stubby grass
is further flattened by roaming sheep,
a wet and muddied path
follows naked hedges
heading down the valley.

To the quiet of a woodland,
where crows and seagulls
swapping swoops, shrieks and squawks
as the blackbirds, robins and sparrows
sound their morning greetings.

Ambling further along the path
frills of milky-white snowdrops
flourish moss-covered tree roots,
with tendered yellow pockets
by cheerful nodding daffodils.

Tribute

With roots buried deep
into earth and water
an ancient beech
still stands firm.
Its once beautiful boughs
are few and bark-beetles
vacated long ago.
Yet, there's a ruggedness
a strength in this bare trunk,
its folklore wisdom on show.

As a sapling it felt
man's vibrations, foot-fall
shouts, explosive bangs
and rustic iron clangs.
Granite hauled on to carts,
the tram's rumble and stutter
echoed through the cutting.
Perhaps, a miner leant
against its trunk, smoking
his little clay pipe.

Out of the old one's roots
another sapling grows,
feeling the rivers flow
flush with heavy rainfall
eroding soft earth banks.
Swirling pools and rapids
breaking over dams

created by nature, the noise
at times, reminiscent
of what its ancestor heard.

A Speckled Woodland

On a pale green leaf
perched so delicately
a resting place
in warm spring sunshine.

A blackbird's song
fills the air
slowly unfolding
its pleated petal wings.

Perhaps it was the breeze
perhaps it was my shadow
but one heartbeat later
it flew off along the hedgerow.

Little Sunshines

I
see the
celandine
awakening,
petals of yellow
gleaming mini sunshine's
lighting up the spring meadow.
As clouds thicken, they slowly close,
dark clouds bring the threatened rain showers.
Now yellow candles light the way homeward.

Summer Acrobats

Scanning clear blue skies
listening intently, I hear
the long high-pitched shrieks
as a swoop of swifts appear.
Like high-speed black boomerangs
zooming through still summer air,
flickering moves that dart and skim
in effortless aerial displays.
A seasonal treasure to savour
before autumn beckons
their return to Africa.

When the wind blows

I read until my eyes sting
ignoring the objections from stiff shoulders
until they grumble then relax in relief
as the lamp is switched off.

Listening to the windows humming,
as westerly winds whip past
slipping beneath the Worm moon,
pulling clouds, darkening the night,
hurling down the river.

Sentries of street lights watching
as seas thump the harbour wall,
and a marina now a symphony of sound.
Its percussion of chatter
and gabbling of water

pester the topsides of yachts.
Below, anchors rumble
dragging across sands
and wind wails through rigging,
where halyards are clanging their masts.

Still the relentless rage of wind
continues its journey over the hills.
Undisturbed at home,
I snuggle down, breathing evenly,
safe in slumber.

The Tavy

Its ancient name was Taui
this infant river
trickles out of moorland
descending through valleys
passing tors and cleave.

The Collybrooke, Wallabrooke
Walkham and Lumburn swell
the Tavy's adventure
jumping over rocks
gushing into pools

squeezing through arches
louder than a stampede,
booming off buildings
cascading over the weir
into a waiting cauldron.

A collar frill forms
full of giant bubbles
that glitter and float
in cream coloured foam
jettisoned over the edge

tumbling over fallen
moss-covered tree trunks,
scattering its flotsam
leaving a trail of lace
drifting on the surface

its pace now slowing
meandering its course
passing people walking
soaking up its energy
the stress of life forgotten.

Devon's Buzzing

A vast bright blue sky and a ruffle
of warm breeze accompanies me.
Through the cooling green hedgerows
filled with vibrant pink valerian,
cream cowslips and honeysuckle
overflowing on to a narrow path.

The meadow is drenched
in a wildflower cocktail of colour
that's a butterfly's delight,
dancing over poppies,
cornflowers, comfrey,
yellow rattle, eye bright
and cat's ear.

Skylarks soar and sing,
swallows swoop down
catching food in flight,
whilst busy bumble bees gather

on thistles and dandelions.
Grasses of cocksfoot, rye and brome
brush my thigh and my fingers graze
their rough and smooth textures.

This is such a far cry
from the frenetic city activity.
So I sit, absorbing this peaceful,
and free summer energy.

Red Kites

I heard them calling
whistling
from one oak tree
to another
to each other
before rising
meeting as one
dancing in the sky.

A Beachcomber's Bounty

As mist lifts along the shore
the soft lilt of retreating tide
leaves behind a curved strand line,
a tangle of seaweed curls
is a beachcomber's lucky dip.
Aged blue mussel and limpet shells,
surfboard-shaped cuttlefish bones,
and an empty crab shell.
Its previous occupant
now acclimatises offshore,
waiting, as its new casing hardens.

A pink sea fan eludes me
but I spot a mermaid's purse,
an oblong leathery pouch
a cradle, that may have held
a baby catfish, ray or shark!

Clambering over jagged rocks,
seawater brightens the colour
of a painted topshell, dog whelk
and yellow periwinkle.
Peering down, I spy a hermit crab.
His little red legs scuttle along
carrying his mobile home,
though he avoids the antlers
of a young tompot blenny
patrolling his hidey-hole.

Looking across the spangled sea
I wonder what surprises, tomorrow
will be thrown back at me?

July in Devon

Like chorus girls
pale green frills of fir trees
wave gaily in morning breezes,
skirts lifting to reveal hundreds
of spindly legs, stretching
back in the deep darkness.
Anonymous tracks, only known
to the night animals, perhaps
a fox follows his pungent
musky scent to take a shortcut.

Staying on the woodland trail,
my footsteps are muffled by
years of compacted pine needles
and fragments of dried leaves.
Chinks of sunlight bathe mauve
rhododendron, capturing sparkles
of early morning dew on grass.
Out of the banks of pink campion,
a silhouette of a young grey

squirrel scampers out. His tail
sparse of fluffiness and small body
disappears into the draping arms
of a weeping willow.
The snap of dead wood alerts
a wood pigeon who flies up,
hiding in an ancient oak.
Two coal tits fly out, reminding me
it's also time to leave.

Shoreline Smash and Grab

The dark choppy seas
make the receding tide jumpy.
Large waves relentlessly
whoosh, roll and pound the shore
attempting a smash and grab.
A deep lumbering, rumbling sound
continuously re-echo as pebbles,
both large and small, resist the pull.
Water hindered by boulders escapes
rushing back to join its mass.

Seagulls benignly perch on high rocks
like spectators at the ringside,
poised and ready to take action.
Lookouts fly over the sea, some land
riding the swells, waiting for a signal,
but fish don't arrive, so as one, they leave.
Though still threatening, the sea retreats
only seaweed, shells and pebbles remain.

They left the beach pristine
but I wonder, as the sun comes out
if at the end of the day,
people will do the same?

Summer's Time

A kestrel glides on the wind
feathers of bright russet and black
outstretched, streamlined, sweeping
over September's yellow gorse,
hiding a little field mouse
who cannot stop his heartbeat
or tiny rapid chest movements.
Easing as danger passes, he scurries
only pausing when a stonechat
no bigger than a redbreast, calls
like two pebbles tapping together.
This loud clacking announcing –
the fields are full of seeds and insects
a feast awaits, come take your fill.

When summer days become shorter
time becomes more precious
to observe what is around us.

Image credited to: wildswimming.co.uk Permission obtained on
18.08.2021.

The Walkham's Healing Song.

Evading Summer's news
of her pending departure,
the shadowed archway
whispers its welcome.
Out of the darkness, light
plays with the high spirits
of fast flowing water.

My cobweb of emotions
skitter around,
like a twig swirling,
caught up in the jumping swells
until latching itself
within a stone harbour.

As I listen to this fluid song
its music soothes,
seeping slowly in
unravelling the tangles.
Quietly resting I watch
as the river rushes on
knowing its work is done.

Autumn's Arrival

Beyond a faded five-bar gate
honey-coloured grasses shimmer
and rattle in the warm wind.
A patchwork of twisting trails
grey strands, flattened by the nomads -
moorland sheep and ponies, who crush
bronzed bracken to graze new grasses.

Peee-u, Peee-u, a lone buzzard mews
until it drifts away over the ridge.
My eye then tracks down the valley
to fall upon a rickety wooden bridge,
where sunlight splinters on river ripples
and its peat-stained water snaking
around the bends in its path.

I climb higher up the hillside
passing swathes of mauve heather
and gorse dressed in yellow.
A family of meadow pippets
fly off in a hurry, perhaps
sensing the change of light
that autumn's equinox brings.

I sit and rest my feet
and bless my good fortune
of seeing the season change.

Untamed Thunder

Spires of fir trees stand aloft
as mist fills the valley basin.
Up on the rocky slopes
wild ponies mosey
munching on clover and grass.
All heads suddenly rise
some whinny in excitement
feeling thunder through their hooves.
He comes, and he's not alone.

A black stallion galloping
a streamlined wild and free spirit
racing ahead of his herd,
surging, urging, up the steep terrain
silky mane lifting, slapping his neck
muscles glistening as hoof-strokes
beat the ground, pounding passed
up beyond the hill
following the falling sun.

Double-Waters

Descending to a wooded valley
misty rain has many birds snuggled down,
I can only hear a buzzard calling
and a pheasant proclaim his domain.

Rain sizzles in the trees, landing
with sounds like popping corn.
Then a grey squirrel scampers and leaps
pausing from his lofty place to peer down.

Forty pairs of amber eyes stare
out of the pink-painted ladies,
some standing with their backs to rain
others carry on grazing.

Every path is layered in yellow, red, green,
gold and brown leaf. Emerald
moss-coated trunks sparkle
feeling soft and spongy to touch.

My footsteps are muffled, squishing
on grass, slurping in mud
and washed in puddles, slipping
over tree roots and wet rocks.

As the two rivers meet, I can feel
its emotional pull.
All I can do is gaze, transfixed
trying to take everything in.

I find a hidden refuge where
copper and cinnamon leaves swirl
free-riding on the river, in circles
that stretch and shrink, 'til pulled into lines.

This life form nips and tugs the river bank
reaching out, my fatigue ebbs away,
a healing energy coursing through me
leaving my burden behind, I can move on.

Haytor

The wildness of Dartmoor is tempered
by lichen-covered rocks,
from the mighty to hand-size pieces
its touch offers solidness to the soul.

As rain feeds the river, so peat-bogs
leeching its hallmark brown stain
seems apt for the dried grasses
and brittle bracken now upon us.

Across the bleak moor, Haytor rests
with clitter haphazardly scattered, as if
giant hands have knocked pieces down
leaving clearings of well-trodden paths.

The quarry, where rusted iron machines
lay abandoned, is now an idyll of tranquillity,
the graceful simplicity of water-lilies
at odds with the untamed brush and trees.

Piled pillows of mauve heather soften
the ravaged landscape, broken up
by an old tramway, lost in times past
but once a thriving industry.

Granite, hewn by feather and tare,
laid down as tracks of carriageway,
for a team of 18-strong horses to pull
flat-topped wagons to waiting barges.

For forty years man and beast
took moorland granite; London Bridge,
the British Museum and Covent Garden Market,
still reap the reward of this toil.

Yet, today, in the rain and sunshine
it feels as if the moor has forgiven us.
Where else can one find such peace
amid this rugged beauty?

A Winter's Walk

Winter's low setting sun
casts light on skeletal branches,
refracting its golden glow
through fringed frail leaves
and clusters of holly berries
bring nature's own fairy lights.

No longer does a fat bumble bee
linger over clover, or bend
a cornflower under its weight.
Its buffet, now the delicate
cream and mauve bloom, peeking
through tightly packed ivy leaves.

Hidden gems reveal themselves
among naked branches:
A nighthawk perches motionless,
nut hatches nestle in holes,
and a windswept woodpecker
bravely digs out insects.

Crows, chacking and cawing
fill twilight skies - like torn black rags.
When stars twinkle, an owl glides
silently on long thin wings
as if rowing across the resting fields,
his sharp eyes searching out supper.

We walk wrapped in nature's shawl
awed by her wondrous display.

Wildflowers in Devon

Memories fade like the tide
washing over yesterday's sand.
Yet, for a while I want to smile
and remember, when your eyes
played games with mine.

Finding your surprises in January
spotting a crocus or snowdrops
scattered on lawns, where sisters
of dog violets nestle in hedgerows
and humble aubretia cling to walls.

February brims with hope
as soft clusters of primroses greet
daisies and wild daffodils, filling
fields and river banks, before calling
upon April's graceful wind flowers.

Together we climb a coast path
overflowing with blackthorn blooms
and chased by hawthorn blossoms.
These plump clouds of white, a backdrop
for butterflies to dance in spring light,
and rest on the vivid yellow of tall gorse.

Next, your bountiful gift of bluebells
choosing dappled woodland to display
the blue and purple hues. Light winds waft
their scents towards regal ragged robins.

June is when wood sorrel shines, as bright
as summer's corn cockle or marigolds.
I delight in how you capture July's meadows,
ablaze with poppies, chicory and cornflowers
where colours shimmer like a fine silk.

Taking shelter under trees from August heat,
we are dwarfed by hedges of foxgloves,
brushed by campions, burdock and nettles -
its sting offset by gifts of sweet blackberries.

As Moorland dresses for its September show
pillows of bell heather fizz in the rain,
their purple and blush pink hues squeezing
extra space amid hip-deep yellow gorse.

As autumn stretches out, the parade begins
watching trees scatter leaves and cover paths
with copper, orange, yellow and gold.

The sunlight, more limited now,
spreads out its fingers for rainbows to form
in droplets and river spray. Winter calls
to hazel catkins, holly and mistletoe,
it's time to stop now, our walk is over.

The year has turned its final page, still
my memory burns bright with images,
thank you for sharing your treasures.

Endorsements

Read Annie Jenkin's poetry collection *Come Walk with Me* and you will feel as if you have accompanied her on one of the many walks around Devon which inspired her verse.

Whether by the sea, or in fields, or woodland, Annie's writing picks you up and places you firmly in the environment. Her words and style, by turns descriptive, distinctive and full of delight, just like Devon itself. And, like all good walks, you will be left feeling positive and relaxed.

Read this slim volume in one sitting, or each poem individually, and you will be transported from the mundane and into the magical, Annie's writing having that rare quality of transforming the familiar into the exotic.

So, come walk with Annie, feel the sun, and the spray, taste the breeze, hear the buzzing and the birdsong, stray from the trodden route, experience the world anew. You won't regret it.

--William Telford, author and journalists, member of Plymouth Atheneum Writers

Annie Jenkin's love for nature shines through every page as she invites us to hike with her through the varied landscapes of Devon. She paints waves, wildflowers and birds for the reader, and invites us to appreciate the moor, mosses, field mise, and rocks "stitched / to the sea" (p.7).

There are touches of humor, and a couple of historical tidbits in this conversational free verse poetry. If you are caught in a "cobweb of emotions" (p.36), you may find that joining Annie in this walk through the English countryside soothing.

--Wilda Morris, author of *Pequod Poems: Gamming with Moby-Dick* and a past president, Illinois State Poetry Society